Apple Watch Guide: The Best Tips & Support Guidebook

by Neo Monefa

Table of Contents

23. THANK YOU FOR READING !

1. From the Box To your Wrist

Set up and pair with iPhone

A setup assistant guides you through a few simple steps to pair Apple Watch with your iPhone and make it your own.

If you have difficulty seeing the Apple Watch or iPhone screen to set it up, VoiceOver or Zoom can help.

- **Set up and pair.** Update your iPhone to iOS software version 8.2 or later (go to Settings > General > Software Update), which includes the companion Apple Watch app. Then open the Apple Watch app on iPhone.

Put Apple Watch on your wrist, then press and hold the side button until you see the Apple logo. When prompted, position your iPhone so that Apple Watch appears in the camera viewfinder on the iPhone screen. Follow the instructions on iPhone and Apple Watch to finish setup. During setup, you'll choose your language, watch orientation, and password.

The Apple Watch App on iPhone

The Apple Watch app on iPhone lets you customize watch settings and options and set up Apple Pay for Apple Watch. It gives you access to the App Store, where you can download and install apps for Apple Watch.

Open the Apple Watch app. On iPhone, tap the Apple Watch app icon, then tap My Watch to open the settings for Apple Watch.

Apple Watch app open on an iPhone to the My Watch screen with options (App Layout, Airplane Mode, Apple Watch, Notifications, Glances, Do Not Disturb, General, Brightness & Text Size, Sounds & Haptics) listed. Scroll down for more. Across the bottom are three tabs. Tap My Watch for access to these settings, tap Explore to find Apple Watch educational videos, and tap App Store to open the App Store to find apps you can get for Apple Watch.

Power on, wake, and unlock

Turn on Apple Watch- If Apple Watch is off, press and hold the side button until the Apple logo appears (you might see a black screen for a short time first), then wait for the watch face.

Turn off Apple Watch- You can power off Apple Watch simply by pressing and holding the side button until the slider appears, then drag it to the right.

Wake Apple Watch- Just raise your wrist or tap the display. Apple Watch sleeps when you lower your wrist. You can also wake Apple Watch by pressing the Digital Crown.

If Apple Watch doesn't wake when you raise your wrist, make sure you've selected the proper wrist and Digital Crown orientation. Open the Settings app (if you're looking at the watch face, press the Digital Crown to get to the Home screen, then tap the Settings icon), go to General > Orientation, then make sure Orientation is set to the wrist you wear Apple Watch on. It's also possible that the battery may need charging.

Wake to the watch face or your last activity- You can set Apple Watch to show the watch face when it wakes, or return you to where you were before it went to sleep. The default is to wake to the watch face. To choose to return to the last app you used, open Settings settings icon, tap General > Activate on Wrist Raise, and make sure Wrist Raise is turned on. Then scroll down to choose opening to the last-used app. You can also do this using the Apple Watch app on iPhone: tap My Watch, go to General > Activate on Wrist Raise, then choose Resume Previous Activity.

Unlock with iPhone- To unlock Apple Watch by entering your iPhone passcode on iPhone, open the Apple Watch app on iPhone, tap My Watch, tap Passcode, then tap Unlock with iPhone. Or, on Apple Watch, open Settings, scroll down, tap Passcode, then turn on Unlock with iPhone.

Note: Your Apple Watch passcode can be different from your iPhone passcode in fact, for security, it's better to make them different.

Enter your passcode- If you take Apple Watch off your wrist or wear it very loosely, it asks for your passcode the next time you try to use it. When the number pad appears, just tap your passcode.

Change the passcode- On Apple Watch, open Settings, scroll down, tap Passcode, then tap Change Passcode and follow the on screen prompts. Enter a new 4-digit passcode, then confirm it. Or open the Apple Watch app on iPhone, tap My Watch, tap Passcode, then tap Change Passcode and follow the on screen prompts.

Turn off the passcode- Open Settings settings icon, tap Passcode, then tap Disable Passcode. Or open the Apple Watch app on iPhone, tap My Watch, tap Passcode, then tap Turn Passcode Off.

Note: If you disable your passcode, you can't use Apple Pay on Apple Watch.

Lock it automatically. Turn on wrist detection to lock your watch automatically when you're not wearing it. Open the Apple Watch app on iPhone, tap My Watch, tap General, then tap Wrist Detection. If you turn on Wrist Detection, you can also see the time when you raise your wrist. If you turn off Wrist Detection, you can't use Apple Pay.

Lock it manually. Press and hold the side button until the sliders appear, then drag the Lock Device slider to the right. You'll be required to enter your passcode the next time you try to use Apple Watch.

You can also put the watch into Power Reserve mode from this screen.

The slider screen with Cancel button in top left and 3 sliders: Power off at top, Power Reserve in middle, and Lock Device at bottom.

Erase Apple Watch data. You can set Apple Watch to erase its data if the incorrect password is entered 10 times. This protects the contents of your watch if it is lost or stolen. Open the Apple Watch app on iPhone, tap My Watch, tap Passcode, then tap Erase Data.

If you forget your passcode. Unpair Apple Watch from its paired iPhone to erase your Apple Watch settings and passcode. You can also reset Apple Watch and pair it again with your iPhone.

Adjust brightness, text size, and sounds

Adjust brightness. Open the Settings app settings icon, then scroll down and tap Brightness & Text Size. Tap a Brightness symbol, then turn the Digital Crown or tap the brightness symbols to adjust. Or open the Apple Watch app on iPhone, tap My Watch, tap Brightness & Text Size, then drag the Brightness slider.

Make the text larger. Open Settings settings icon, then scroll down and tap Brightness & Text Size. Tap Text Size, then tap the letters or scroll the Digital Crown to increase or decrease the text size. Or open the Apple Watch app on iPhone, tap My Watch, tap Brightness & Text Size, and drag the Text Size slider.

Make the text bold. Open Settings settings icon, then scroll down and tap Brightness & Text Size. Turn on Bold Text. Or open the Apple Watch app on iPhone, tap My Watch, tap Brightness & Text Size, then turn on Bold Text.

When you turn on bold text from either Apple Watch or your paired iPhone, Apple Watch must reset to apply the change. Tap Continue.

Adjust sound. Open Settings settings icon, then scroll down and tap Sounds & Haptics. Tap the volume buttons under Ringer and Alert Sounds or tap the slider once to select it, then turn the Digital Crown to adjust the volume. Or open the Apple Watch app on iPhone, tap My Watch, tap Sounds & Haptics, then drag the Ringer and Alert Sounds slider.

Sounds & Haptics settings screen on Apple Watch. Turn the Digital Crown or tap the volume symbols to increase or decrease the volume of ringers and alerts. Tap Mute to mute Apple Watch.
Mute Apple Watch. Open Settings Settings icon, scroll down and tap Sounds & Haptics, then turn on Mute. Or swipe up on the watch face, swipe to the Settings glance, then tap the Mute button. You can also open the Apple Watch app on iPhone, tap My Watch, tap Sounds & Haptics, then turn on Mute.

The Settings glance where you can see the connection status of your watch and iPhone and set Airplane mode, Do Not Disturb, and Mute. You can also ping your iPhone. Mute is selected.
You can also quickly mute new alert and notification sounds by resting the palm of your hand on the watch display and holding it there for at least three seconds. You'll feel a tap to confirm that mute is on. You must first turn on the option in the Apple Watch app on iPhone. Tap My Watch, tap Sounds & Haptics, then turn on Cover to Mute.

Adjust haptic intensity. Apple Watch taps your wrist for certain notifications and alerts, and you can adjust the intensity of these haptics. Open Settings settings icon, then scroll down and tap Sounds & Haptics. Tap the haptic buttons under Ringer and Alert Haptics or tap the slider once to select it, then turn the Digital Crown to adjust the haptic intensity. Or open the Apple Watch app on iPhone, tap My Watch, tap Sounds & Haptics, then drag the Ringer and Alert Haptics slider.

Sounds & Haptics settings screen where you can scroll down to Ringer and Alert Haptics, then tap the haptic symbols to increase or decrease the intensity of taps.
Do Not Disturb is an easy way to silence Apple Watch. It keeps calls and alerts (except for alarms) from making any sounds or lighting up the screen.

Turn on Do Not Disturb. Swipe up on the watch face, swipe left or right to the Settings glance, then tap the Do Not Disturb button Do Not Disturb icon. Or open Settings settings icon, tap Do Not Disturb, then turn on Do Not Disturb. When Do Not Disturb is on, you'll see the Do Not Disturb icon at the top of the screen.

Two Apple Watch screens showing two ways to set Do Not Disturb: in the Settings glance or in the Settings app.
To silence both Apple Watch and iPhone, open the Apple Watch app on iPhone, tap My Watch, and turn on Do Not Disturb > Mirror iPhone. Then, any time you change Do Not Disturb on one, the other will change to match.

Change the language and orientation

Change language or region format. Open the Apple Watch app on iPhone, tap My Watch, then go to General > Language & Region.

Set the system language in the Apple Watch app: Go to My Watch, then General, then Language & Region. Tap System Language to change it.
Switch wrists or change the Digital Crown orientation. If you want to switch wrists or prefer to orient the Digital Crown differently, adjust your orientation settings so that raising your wrist wakes Apple Watch, and turning the Digital Crown moves things in the

direction you expect. Open the Settings app the Settings icon, then go to General > Orientation. To change the settings in the Apple Watch app on iPhone, tap My Watch, then go to General > Watch Orientation.

Side by side screens showing the Orientation settings on Apple Watch and the same settings in the Apple Watch app on iPhone. You can set your wrist and digital crown preference.

Charge Apple Watch

Charge Apple Watch. In a well-ventilated area, place the included Apple Watch Magnetic Charging Cable or Apple Watch Magnetic Charging Case on a flat surface, plug it into the included power adapter, or a power adapter you use with iPhone or iPad, and then plug it into a power outlet. When using the Apple Watch Magnetic Charging Case, keep the case open. Position the back of Apple Watch on the charger. The magnets on the charger align Apple Watch properly, and you'll hear a chime (unless Apple Watch is muted) and see a charging symbol on the watch face. The symbol is red when Apple Watch needs power and turns green charging icon when Apple Watch is charging.

Check remaining power. On Apple Watch, swipe up on the watch face, then swipe to the Battery glance.

You can also add the battery indicator to many of the watch faces, including Modular, Color, Utility, Simple, Chronograph, and Mickey Mouse. With the watch face showing, firmly press the display, tap Customize, then swipe to the left until you can choose individual feature locations. Tap a location, turn the Digital Crown to choose Battery, then press the Digital Crown to exit.

Use Power Reserve to stretch available power. You can put Apple Watch in Power Reserve mode to save power when the battery is low. Apple Watch continues to keep and display time, but other apps aren't available for use. Swipe up on the watch face, swipe to the Power glance, tap Power Reserve, then tap Proceed. You can also press the side button until you see the slider appear, then drag it to the right.

Two ways to turn on Power Reserve. Swipe to the Power glance or press and hold the side button to bring up the screen with three sliders: the middle one is Power Reserve.

Note: Apple Watch automatically enters Power Reserve mode if the percentage of battery charge remaining drops below approximately 10 percent.

Return to normal power mode. Press and hold the side button to restart Apple Watch. There must be sufficient charge in the battery for this to work.

Check time since last charge. Open the Apple Watch app on iPhone, tap My Watch, then go to General > Usage, where you can view the Usage and Standby values. These values, added together, give you the elapsed time since the last full charge.

On the Usage screen in the Apple Watch app, view power values for Usage, Standby, and Power Reserve in the bottom half of the screen.

2. The Basics

Use and organize apps

Apple Watch includes apps for a variety of communication, information, and timekeeping tasks. They're on a single Home screen, where you can arrange them as you like.

Open an App. From the watch face, press the Digital Crown to get to the Home screen, then tap the app icon. Or turn the Digital Crown to open whichever app is in the center of the Home screen.

Return to the last app. Double-click the Digital Crown.

Return to the watch face. Tap the watch icon watch icon on the Home screen to return to your watch face. Or press the Digital Crown.

Rearrange your apps. On Apple Watch, press the Digital Crown to go to the Home screen. Touch and hold an app until the apps jiggle and the app icons look the same size, then drag the app you want to move to a new location. Press the Digital Crown when you're done.

The Layout screen on the Apple Watch app on iPhone, showing the apps layout. Touch and drag to move apps around.
Find and install apps from the App Store. Open the Apple Watch app on iPhone, then tap App Store to find apps for Apple Watch. Purchase, download, and install apps on your iPhone. On Apple Watch, you'll see a message prompting you to install the app. Tap Yes.

Bottom of the Apple Watch app screen on iPhone, showing three tabs: the left tab is My Watch where you go for Apple Watch settings, the middle tab lets you explore Apple Watch videos, and the right tab takes you to the App Store, where you can download apps for Apple Watch.

Adjust settings for installed apps. Open the Apple Watch app on iPhone, tap My Watch, and scroll down to view your apps. Tap an app name to change its settings.

Check storage used by apps. Open the Apple Watch app on iPhone, tap My Watch, then go to General > Usage. View the storage used by each app and the available storage left on Apple Watch.

Hide an installed app from Apple Watch. On the Home screen, touch and hold the app icon until you see an X on the border. Tap the X to remove the app from Apple Watch. It remains installed on your paired iPhone, unless you delete it from there. To show or hide installed apps on Apple Watch, open the Apple Watch app on iPhone, tap My Watch, scroll down to see apps you've installed, tap the app name, and then tap Show App on Apple Watch. You can't hide the apps that came with Apple Watch. For information on showing or hiding glances, see Check your glances.

Get in touch with friends
The side button on Apple Watch gives you quick access to people you stay in touch with the most. Press the side button, pick a friend, then call, send a message, or use Digital Touch. But first, add your friends to Apple Watch.

- **Add friends to Apple Watch on iPhone.** Apple Watch automatically adds up to 12 of your favorite contacts from iPhone. To change the list of friends that appears on Apple Watch, open the Apple Watch app, tap My Watch, then tap Friends. In the Friends list, tap Add Friend, then tap your friend in the list of contacts that appears. If your friend isn't in the list, open the Contacts app on iPhone and add them, then try again.

- **See friends on Apple Watch.** Press the side button to see up to 12 of your friends. Turn the Digital Crown to highlight each friend. Tap a friend's picture or initials, then choose how you want to get in touch.

Use Handoff to move between Apple Watch and iPhone

The Handoff feature on Apple Watch and iPhone lets you move from device to device without losing focus on what you're doing. For example, you can easily check email on Apple Watch, but you might want to switch to iPhone to type a reply using the onscreen keyboard. Simply wake iPhone, and you see an icon in the lower-left corner of the Lock screen that matches the app you're using on Apple Watch—for example, Mail. Swipe up on the icon to open the same email on iPhone, then finish your reply.

You can use Handoff with these apps: Mail, Maps, Messages, Phone, Reminders, and Calendar, as well as Siri. For Handoff to work, your Apple Watch must be in close proximity to your iPhone.

When you want to read a message on iPhone, select it on Apple Watch and then swipe the mail icon up in the bottom left corner of the lock screen on iPhone.
Turn Handoff on or off. Open the Apple Watch app on iPhone, tap My Watch, then turn on General > Enable Handoff.

Locate your iPhone

Misplaced your iPhone? Apple Watch can help you find it if it's nearby.

Ping your iPhone. Swipe up on the watch face, swipe to the Settings glance, then tap the Ping iPhone button.

The Settings glance where you can see the connection status of your watch and iPhone and set Airplane mode, Do Not Disturb, and Mute. You can also ping your iPhone. Ping iPhone is selected.
If iPhone is not in range of Apple Watch, you can also try to find it using Find My iPhone from iCloud.com.

Use Apple Watch without its paired iPhone

Although you need an iPhone to do most things with Apple Watch, you can still do several things with Apple Watch without having an iPhone in range.

Play music from a synced playlist on Apple Watch

Use the watch, alarms, timers, and the stopwatch

Keep track of your activity (stand, move, exercise) with the Activity Activity icon app

Track workouts

Display photos from synced photo albums

Use Apple Pay to make purchases. See Make purchases with Apple Pay.

Three Apple Watch screens showing options for using the watch without the companion iPhone nearby: playing music, checking activity progress, and running screen shows elapsed time of workout. Apple Watch uses Bluetooth wireless technology to connect to its paired iPhone and uses the iPhone for many wireless functions. Apple Watch can't configure new Wi-Fi networks on its own, but it can connect to Wi-Fi networks you've set up on the paired iPhone.

If your Apple Watch and iPhone are on the same network but aren't connected by Bluetooth, you can also do the following on Apple Watch without iPhone:

Send and receive messages using iMessage

Send and receive Digital Touch messages

Use Siri

Siri on Apple Watch

Siri can perform tasks and deliver lots of information right on Apple Watch.

Ask Siri a question. Just raise Apple Watch or tap the screen. When it wakes, say "Hey, Siri" followed by your request. You can also press and hold the Digital Crown until you see the listening indicator at the bottom of the screen, then say your request and release the Digital Crown. To reply to a question from Siri or just continue the conversation, hold down the Digital Crown and speak. Or simply say "Hello, Siri" and your request.

3. Watch Faces

Customize your watch face

You can customize the Apple Watch face so it looks the way you want and provides the functions you need. Choose from a variety of watch face designs, adjust colors, features, and other details, then add it to your collection so you can switch when you need the right timekeeping tools—or whenever you'd like a change.

Change the watch face. With the watch face showing, firmly press the display, then swipe to see the faces in your collection. When you find the face you want, tap it.

What you see when you firmly press the watch face. You can swipe left or right to see other watch face options. Tap customize for a watch face to add the features you want.
You can add special functions to your watch face, so you can instantly check things like stock prices or the weather report.

Add features to the watch face. With the watch face showing, firmly press the display, then tap Customize. Swipe to select a feature, then turn the Digital Crown to adjust. On some faces, you need to tap a feature to select it. When you're finished, press the Digital Crown to save your changes. Tap the face to switch to it. For more information about each watch face, see Watch faces and features.

Utility watch face on the left. Tap Customize button. Customize screen on the right with clock detail feature highlighted. Turn the crown to change options.
Add a watch face to your collection. Assemble your own collection of custom faces even different versions of the same design. With the current watch face showing, firmly press the display, swipe all the way to the right, then tap the New button (+). Swipe up and down to browse designs, then tap the one you want to add. After you add it, you can customize it.

New watch face screen. Tap watch face to swipe up and down for designs. Tap to add one.
Delete a face from your collection. Don't use a face much anymore? With the current watch face showing, firmly press the display, swipe to the face you don't want, then swipe it up and tap Delete. You can always add the watch face again later.

Watch face showing. Swipe up to delete watch face.
Advance the watch time. Like to set your watch ahead? Open the Settings app Settings icon, tap Time, tap +0 min, then turn the Digital Crown to set the watch ahead by as much as 59 minutes. This setting only changes the time shown on the watch face it doesn't affect alarms, times in notifications, or any other times (such as World Clock).

In the Time settings app, turn the Digital Crown to increase the time you want displayed on your watch face.

Watch faces and features

Apple Watch includes a variety of watch faces, any of which you can customize to suit you. Check frequently for software updates; the set of watch faces that follows might differ from what you see on your Apple Watch.

Astronomy
This Astronomy watch face shows you the solar system and the exact position of the planets, sun, and moon, and displays the day, date, and current time. The Astronomy watch face, which displays the day, date, and current time, which you can't change. You can view the Earth, Moon, or solar system on the watch face and tap the screen to see positions of the planets, phases of the moon, and more.

Chronograph
This watch face measures time in precise increments, like a classic analog stopwatch. It includes a stopwatch, which can be activated right from the face. The Chronograph watch face, where you can adjust the face color and details of the dial. You can also add these features to it: date, calendar, moon phase, sunrise/sunset, weather,

stocks, activity summary, alarm, timer, battery percentage, and world clock. The watch face also includes a stopwatch.

Color
This watch face displays the time and any features you add in your choice of bright colors.
The Color watch face, where you can adjust the color of the watch face and add these features to it: calendar/date, moon phase, sunrise/sunset, weather, activity, alarm, timer, stopwatch, battery percentage, world clock, and your monogram
Adjust basic characteristics: Dial color

Add to the watch face: Date • Moon phase • Sunrise/sunset • Weather • Activity summary • Alarm • Timer • Stopwatch • Battery charge • World Clock • Your monogram (displays initials above the center; initials are taken from your Contacts information)

Mickey Mouse
Let Mickey Mouse give you a whimsical view of time, and watch his foot tap off the seconds.
The Mickey Mouse watch face where you can add these features: Date, Calendar, Moon phase, Sunrise/sunset, Weather, Activity summary, Alarm, Timer, Stopwatch, Battery charge, World clock, Expanded views of all the preceding features plus Stocks.
Add to the watch face: Date • Calendar • Moon phase • Sunrise/sunset • Weather • Activity summary • Alarm • Timer • Stopwatch • Battery charge • World Clock • Expanded views of all the preceding features plus Stocks

Modular
The Modular watch face has a flexible grid design that lets you add many features to give you thorough view of your day. The Modular watch face, where you can adjust the color of the watch face. You can also add these features to it: calendar/date, moon phase, sunrise/sunset, weather, stocks, activity, alarm, timer, stopwatch, battery percentage, world clock, next meeting, and moon phase details.
Adjust basic characteristics: Color

Add to the watch face: Date • Calendar • Moon phase • Sunrise/Sunset • Weather • Stocks • Activity summary • Alarm • Timer • Stopwatch • Battery charge • World Clock • Expanded views of Calendar, Weather, Stocks, Activity, Alarm, Timer, Stopwatch, and World Clock

Motion
The Motion watch face displays a beautiful animated theme-butterflies, flowers, or jellyfish.
The Motion watch face, where you can choose the object in motion and add these features to the watch face: date, with or without day.
Adjust basic characteristic: The animated butterfly, flower, or jellyfish
Add to the watch face: Date (with or without day)

Simple
This minimalistic and elegant watch face lets you add detail to the dial and features to the corners.
The Simple watch face, where you can adjust the color of the sweep hand and adjust the numbering and detail of the dial. You can also add these features to it: moon phase, sunrise/sunset, weather, activity, alarm, timer, stopwatch, battery percentage, world clock, and date.
Adjust basic characteristics: Color of the sweep hand • Detail and numbering of the dial

Add to the watch face: Date • Calendar • Moon phase • Sunrise/Sunset • Weather • Activity summary • Alarm • Timer • Stopwatch • Battery charge • World Clock

Solar
Based on your current location and time of day, the Solar watch face displays the sun's position in the sky, as well as the day, date, and current time.
The Solar watch face displays the day, date, and current time, which can't be modified. Turn the crown to move the sun in the sky to dusk, dawn, zenith, sunset, and darkness.

Utility

This watch face is practical and functional; add up to three features to display what you want to see at a glance.

The Utility watch face, where you can adjust the color of the sweep hand and adjust the numbering and detail of the dial. You can also add these features to it: Date, Calendar, Moon phase, Sunrise/sunset, Weather, Activity summary, Alarm, Timer, Stopwatch, Battery charge, World clock, Expanded views of all the preceding features plus Stocks.

Adjust basic characteristics: Color of the second hand • Detail and number of the dial

Add to the watch face: Date • Calendar • Moon phase • Sunrise/Sunset • Weather • Activity summary • Alarm • Timer • Stopwatch • Battery charge • World Clock • Expanded views of all the preceding features plus Stocks

X-Large

The X-Large watch face displays the time in digital format, filling the screen. You can change the color.

Adjust basic characteristics: Color

4. Notifications

Notifications on Apple Watch

Apps send notifications to keep you informed-- meeting invitations, messages, and exercise reminders are just a few examples. Notifications are displayed on Apple Watch as soon as they arrive. If you don't read them right away, they're saved so you can check them later.

Respond to live notifications

Respond to a notification when it arrives. If you hear or feel a notification, raise Apple Watch to view it. Turn the Digital Crown to scroll to the bottom of the notification, then tap a button there. Or tap the app icon in the notification to open the corresponding app.

Dismiss a notification. Swipe down on the notification you're reading, or scroll to the bottom of the notification and tap Dismiss.

Choose which notifications you get. On iPhone, go to Settings > Notifications to specify which apps and events generate notifications. Then, open the Apple Watch app on iPhone, tap My Watch, tap Notifications, tap the app (for example, Messages), then choose Mirror my iPhone. Or, to choose different notification settings than those on iPhone, choose Custom instead.

Sources of notifications are listed in the Apple Watch app in iPhone. Tap My Watch, tap Notifications, then scroll down.
Silence notifications. To silence notifications on Apple Watch, swipe up on the watch face, swipe to the Settings glance, then tap Silent Mode. You'll still feel a tap when a notification arrives. To prevent sound or tap, tap Do Not Disturb.

Keep it private. When you raise your wrist to see a notification, you get a quick summary, then full details a few seconds later. For example, when a message arrives, you see who it's from first, then the message appears. To stop the full notification from appearing unless you tap it, open the Apple Watch app on iPhone, tap My Watch, tap Notifications, then turn on Notification Privacy.

Respond to unread notifications

See notifications you haven't responded to. If you don't respond to a notification when it arrives, it's saved in Notification Center. A red dot at the top of your watch face shows you have an unread notification-- swipe down to view it. To scroll the notifications list, swipe up or down or turn the Digital Crown.

A red dot appears above the twelve o'clock position on your watch face when you have a notification to attend to. Swipe down to view. Respond to a notification in the list. Tap the notification.

Clear notifications. Apple Watch removes notifications from the list when you tap to read them. To delete a notification without reading it, swipe it to the left, then tap Clear. To clear all notifications, firmly press the display, then tap Clear All.

The Clear button appears to the right of a notification when you swipe the notification to the left.

5. Glances

Get a quick glance at useful information

From the watch face, you have quick access to Glances-- scannable summaries of the information you view most frequently. Swipe up on the watch face to see glances, then swipe left or right to see different glances.

Organize your glances
See only what you want to see. To choose your glances, open the Apple Watch app on iPhone, tap My Watch, tap Glances, then remove or include glances. (You can't remove the Settings glance.)

Put them in handy order. Open the Apple Watch app on iPhone, tap My Watch, tap Glances, then drag the reorder buttons.

6. Keeping the Time

Check the time in other locations

The World Clock. This app on Apple Watch lets you check the time in cities around the globe. Open the app to check times at other locations, or add cities to your watch face for quick reference.

You can ask Siri what time it is in any city in the world.
Check the time in another city. Open World Clock World Clock icon, then turn the Digital Crown or swipe the screen to scroll the list. If there's a city whose time you'd always like to see, you can add the world clock to your watch face and choose the city to display.

See additional information. To see more information about a city, including time of sunrise and sunset, tap the city in the World Clock list. When you're finished, tap < in the upper left, or swipe right to return to the city list. As always, you can press the Digital Crown to return to the watch face.

World Clock app more info screen showing New York current time, time difference from your city, and sunrise/sunset times. Tap screen or press crown to return to city list.
Add a city to World Clock. The cities you add on iPhone appear in World Clock World Clock icon on Apple Watch. Open the Clock app on iPhone, tap World Clock, then tap the Add button (+).

Screen of the Clock app on iPhone, where you can add cities to the World Clock app.
Add a world clock to your watch face. You can add a world clock to several watch faces—some faces let you add more than one. Firmly press the display, then tap Customize. Swipe left until you can select individual face features, tap the one you'd like to use for a world clock, then turn the Digital Crown to choose a city. When you're finished, press the Digital Crown. You can add a world clock to these faces: Chronograph, Color, Mickey Mouse, Modular, Simple, and Utility.

Two watch screens: one shows adding another city time to the watch face, and the other shows the time displayed on the watch face. Change city abbreviations. If you want to change a city abbreviation used on Apple Watch, open the Apple Watch app on iPhone, tap My Watch, then go to Clock > City Abbreviations. Tap any city to change its abbreviation.

Watch face with pointer to the time in London, using the abbreviation LON. The next screen shows the option in the Apple Watch on iPhone where you can modify the abbreviation of cities.

Set alarms

Use the Alarm Clock app alarm icon to play a sound or vibrate Apple Watch at the right time. You can also add an alarm to your watch face, so you can see upcoming alarms at a glance—and open the Alarm Clock app with a tap.

You can ask Siri to set a repeating alarm for the time of your choice. Add an alarm. Open Alarm Clock alarm icon, firmly press the display, then tap New +. Tap Change Time, tap AM or PM, tap the hours or minutes, turn the Digital Crown to adjust, then tap Set. Tap < in the upper left to return to the alarm settings, then set repeat, label, and snooze to suit you.

Five watch screens showing the process for adding an alarm: Press to add alarm, turn Digital Crown to set the time, set options in settings, set repeat options, and turn on Snooze.
Set or adjust an alarm. Open Alarm Clock alarm icon, then tap the alarm in the list to change its settings. Tap next to the alarm to turn it on or off.

Alarms screen with three alarms and switches to turn them on or off. You can tell Siri to turn off a specific alarm.
See the upcoming alarm on your watch face. With the watch face showing, firmly press the display, then tap Customize. Swipe left until you can select individual face features, tap the one you'd like to use for alarms, then turn the Digital Crown to choose the alarm.

When you're finished, press the Digital Crown. You can add alarms to these faces: Chronograph, Color, Mickey Mouse, Modular, Simple, and Utility.

Two screens, one showing how you set an option to add an alarm to your watch face, the other showing the alarm time displayed on the watch face.
Don't let yourself snooze. When an alarm sounds, you can tap Snooze to wait several minutes before the alarm sounds again. If you don't want to allow snooze, tap the alarm in the list of alarms, then turn off Snooze.

Two watch screens, one showing a watch face with an alarm snooze button. The other shows the Edit Alarm settings, where you can turn Snooze on or off.
Delete an alarm. Open Alarm Clock alarm icon, tap the alarm in the list, scroll to the bottom, then tap Delete.

Edit alarm screen, where you scroll to the bottom to delete an alarm.

Use a timer

The Timer app timer icon on Apple Watch can help you keep track of time. Set timers up to 24 hours.

You can ask Siri to set a timer for up to 24 hours.
Set a timer. Open Timer timer icon, tap hours or minutes, turn the Digital Crown to adjust, then tap Start.

Tap hours or minutes and turn the Digital Crown to set a timer.
Set a timer for longer than 12 hours. While adjusting the timer, firmly press the display, then tap 24.

In the Timer settings, you can choose between 12 and 24 hour display and set a timer for a longer period of time.
Add a timer to your watch face. If you use a timer often, add a timer to your watch face. With the watch face showing, firmly press the display, then tap Customize. Swipe left until you can select individual face features, tap the one you'd like to use for the timer,

then turn the Digital Crown to choose the timer. When you're finished, press the Digital Crown. You can add a timer to these faces: Chronograph, Color, Mickey Mouse, Modular, Simple, and Utility.

Two screens show modifying a watch face to include the timer, and the other screen shows the finished effect of having the timer on the watch face.

Time events with a stopwatch

Time events with accuracy and ease. Apple Watch can time full events (up to 11 hours, 55 minutes) and keep track of lap or split times, then show the results as a list, a graph, or live on your watch face. The Chronograph watch face has the stopwatch built in, and you can add a stopwatch to these faces: Color, Mickey Mouse, Modular, Simple, and Utility.

Switch to the stopwatch. Open the Stopwatch app stopwatch icon, or tap the stopwatch on your watch face (if you've added it or you're using the Chronograph watch face).

Three ways to use a stopwatch: use a digital stopwatch in the app, use an analog stopwatch in the app, add stopwatch controls to your Chronograph watch face.
Start, stop, and reset. Tap the Start button. Tap the Lap button to record a lap or split. Tap the Stop button to record the final time. Timing continues while you switch back to the watch face or open other apps. When you finish, tap the Reset button or the Lap button to reset.

On the analog stopwatch, tap the left button to start and stop it, and the right button to record lap times.
Choose the stopwatch format. You can change the format of the timing display before, after, or during timing. Firmly press the display while the stopwatch is showing, then tap Analog, Digital, Graph, or Hybrid.

While using Apple Watch as a stopwatch, press the display to change the format. Choose Analog, Digital, Graph, or Hybrid. Switch between analog 1-dial and 3-dial with splits. Swipe up on the 1-dial analog stopwatch display to see separate minute, second, and tenths dials above a scrolling list of lap times.

Screen of a stopwatch showing a 3-dial option with splits. Review results. Review results on the display you used for timing, or change displays to analyze your lap times and fastest/slowest laps (marked with green and red) in the format you prefer. If the display includes a list of lap times, turn the Digital Crown to scroll.

Monitor timing from the watch face. To keep an eye on a timing session while displaying your regular watch face, add a stopwatch to the face. Your current elapsed time will be visible on the face, and you can tap it to switch to the Stopwatch app stopwatch icon and check your lap times.

You can add a stopwatch to your watch face and tap it to open the Stopwatch app.
Quit using the stopwatch. If you're using the Stopwatch app stopwatch icon, just press the Digital Crown. If you're using the Chronograph watch face, the stopwatch controls are always on the face-- tap the Lap button to reset.

7. Messages

Read and reply to messages

You can read incoming text messages right on Apple Watch. You can also reply from Apple Watch, by dictating or choosing a prepared response, or switch to iPhone to type a response.

Read a message. You'll feel a notification tap or hear an alert sound when a message arrives—just raise Apple Watch to read it. Turn the Digital Crown to scroll.

Open a conversation in the Messages app. Tap the Messages icon Messages icon in the notification.

See a photo in the message. Tap the photo to view it, double-tap it to fill the screen, and drag it to pan. When you're finished, swipe left from the edge of the photo screen to return to the conversation. If you want to save the photo, open the message in the Messages app on iPhone, and save it there.

Listen to an audio clip in a message. Tap the clip to listen. The clip is deleted after two minutes to save space-- if you want to keep it, tap Keep below the clip. The audio will remain for 30 days, and you can set it to remain longer on iPhone: go to Settings > Messages, scroll to Audio Messages, tap Expire, then tap a value.

View a video in a message. In the Messages app Messages icon, tap a video in a message to start playing the video full-screen. Tap once to display the playback controls. Double-tap to zoom out and turn the Digital Crown to adjust the volume. Swipe or tap the back button to return to the conversation.

Jump to the top of a long message. In Messages Messages icon, tap the top of the display.

Reply to a message. If the message just arrived, tap its notification, turn the Digital Crown to scroll to the bottom of the message, then tap Reply. If it arrived a while ago, swipe down on the watch face to see the message notification, tap it, then scroll to the bottom and tap the Reply button. To mark the message as read, tap Dismiss or swipe the message. Press the Digital Crown to dismiss the notification without marking the message as read.

Tap a message to reply to it.

Decide how to be notified. Open the Apple Watch app on iPhone, tap My Watch, then tap Messages. Tap Custom to set options for how you want to be notified when you receive a message.

Messages screen in Apple Watch app on iPhone. You can customize your alerts and choose to show them, turn on sound, turn on haptic, and filter the alerts you want to see.

Send and manage messages

Send a new message. Open Messages Messages icon, firmly press the list of conversations, then tap the New Message icon. Tap a contact in the list of recent conversations that appears, tap + in the lower left to choose from your full list of contacts, or tap the Microphone button to search for someone in your contacts or to dictate a phone number. There are six ways to compose your message:

1) Use preset replies

2) Dictate new text

3) Record an audio clip

4) Send an animated emoji

5) Send a map showing your location (if you have your iPhone with you)

6) Switch to iPhone and use the full keyboard to type a message

Send a preset reply. When replying to a message, you see a list of handy phrases that you can use-- just tap one to send it. The phrases include contextual responses based on the last message received and six default phrases that you can change. To substitute your own phrases, open the Apple Watch app on iPhone, tap My Watch, go to Messages > Default Replies, then tap a default reply to change it.

If the preset replies aren't in the language you want to use, you can change them by switching to the keyboard for that language in the same conversation in Messages on iPhone. Cancel your original reply on Apple Watch, then reply again to see the replies in the new language. If you don't want to change keyboards, you can dictate and send an audio clip in the language of your choice.

Messages screen showing Cancel button at top, three preset replies ("What's up?", "I'm on my way.", and "OK."). Two buttons at bottom: Emoji and Microphone.
Dictate text. While creating a message or reply, tap the Microphone button microphone icon, say what you want to say, then tap Done. Don't forget that you can speak punctuation, too (for example, "did it arrive question mark"). You can choose to send the message as a text message or an audio clip-- just tap your choice. If you choose audio clip, the recipient gets a voice message to listen to, not a text message to read.

If you use more than one language and your dictation isn't transcribed in the right language for a conversation, you can still send it as an audio clip. To change the dictation language, change the Siri language on iPhone in Settings > General > Siri, then start a new conversation.

Messages screen showing conversation. Last response is an audio message with a play button.
Always send dictated text as an audio clip. If you like to send all your dictated text as an audio clip, you don't need to choose it every time-- open the Apple Watch app on iPhone, tap My Watch, go to Messages > Audio Messages, then tap an option.

Include animated emoji. While creating a message or reply, tap the Emoji button emoji button, then swipe to browse available images. Turn the Digital Crown to scroll and modify the image (to turn the smile into a frown, for example). On faces, drag left or right across the eyes or mouth to change the expression further. To see other types of images, swipe to the next pages. The last page lists traditional emoji. When you find the right symbol, tap it to add it to your message, then tap Send.

Messages screen with emoji in center. You can scroll to change the expression and see more variations on the theme.
Share your location. To send someone a map showing your current location, firmly press the display while viewing the conversation, then tap Send Location.

Messages screen showing a map of the sender's location. Firmly press display to send your location in a conversation.
Note: On your paired iPhone, make sure Share My Location is turned on in Settings > iCloud > Share My Location.

View message details. Firmly press the display while viewing the conversation, then tap Details to see the contact information of the other participant(s) in the conversation. Or swipe left on the conversation, then tap Details.

Delete a conversation. Swipe left on the conversation, tap Trash, then tap Trash to confirm.

8. Digital Touch

Send a Digital Touch

Send a sketch, a pattern of taps. In the illustrations that follow, the image on the left shows what is sent, and the image on the right shows the notification received.

To experience a Digital Touch someone has sent, just tap a notification.

Send a sketch. Draw on the screen.

Tap the color button in the top right corner to change the color of your sketches.
Send a tap. Tap the screen to send a single tap or tap repeatedly to send a tap pattern.

You can even send your heartbeat to a friend. Place two fingers on the display until you feel your heartbeat and see it animated on the screen.

9. Mailbox

Read mail

Read mail in the Mail app. On Apple Watch, open the Mail app Mail icon, turn the Digital Crown to scroll the message list, then tap a message. To read the message or reply on iPhone, just swipe up on the Mail icon in the lower-left corner of the iPhone Lock screen.

When you want to read a message on iPhone, select it on Apple Watch and then swipe the mail icon up in the bottom left corner of the lock screen on iPhone.

Read mail in a notification. If you set Apple Watch to show mail notifications, you can read a new message right in the notification. Tap the notification when it first appears, or swipe down on the watch face later to see notifications you've received, then tap a mail notification. To dismiss the notification, swipe down from the top or tap Dismiss at the end of the message.

If you don't receive notifications for mail, go to Settings > Notifications on iPhone and check to see if you have notifications turned on for Mail.

Note: Apple Watch supports most text styles and some formats; quoted text appears in a different color rather than as an indentation. If you receive an HTML message with complex elements, Apple Watch tries to display a text alternative of the message. Try reading the message on your iPhone instead.

Switch to iPhone. Some messages are easier to read in full on iPhone—wake iPhone, then swipe up on the Mail icon in the lower left corner of the lock screen.

Go back to the top of a long mail message. Turn the Digital Crown to scroll quickly, or just tap the top of the display.

Scroll to read a long message and tap the top of the display to quickly return to the top of the message.
Open Phone or Maps. Tap a phone number in a mail message to open Phone phone icon, or an address to open Maps Maps icon.

Reply to email. You need to use iPhone to compose a reply-- just wake iPhone and swipe up on the mail icon in the lower-left corner of the Lock screen.

Manage mail

Flag a mail message. If you're reading the message in Mail on Apple Watch, firmly press the display, then tap Flag. If you're looking at the message list, swipe left on the message, then tap More. You can also flag the message when you preview it in a notification-- swipe to the Flag button at the bottom of the message. You can unflag a message that's already been flagged.

Press the display when you're reading a message on Apple Watch to mark it as Unread, Flag it, or send it to the trash.

Note: If you swipe left on a message thread, the action you choose (Flag, Mark as Unread, or Delete) applies to the entire thread.

Change the flag style. Open the Apple Watch app on iPhone, tap My Watch, then go to Mail > Custom > Flag Style.

Mark email as read or unread. Firmly press the display, then tap Unread or Read. If you're looking at the message list, swipe left on the message, then tap More.

Delete email. Firmly press the display, then tap Trash. If you're looking at the message list, swipe left on the message, then tap Trash. You can also delete a message from its notification—scroll to the bottom of the message, then tap Trash.

Note: If your account is set to archive messages, you'll see an Archive button instead of a Trash button.

Choose which mailbox appears on Apple Watch. Open the Apple Watch app on iPhone, tap My Watch, then go to Mail > Include Mail. You can specify only one mailbox, although if you don't choose a mailbox, you'll see content from all inboxes.

Customize alerts. Open the Apple Watch app on iPhone, tap My Watch, then turn on Mail > Show Alerts. Tap each account or group, turn on the option to be alerted, then choose Sound or Haptic.

If your message list is too long. To make your mail list more compact, you can reduce the number of lines of preview text shown for each email in the list. Open the Apple Watch app on iPhone, tap My Watch, go to Mail > Message Preview, then choose to show 2 lines of the message, 1 line, or none.

10. Phone Calls

Answer phone calls

Answer a call. When you feel the incoming call notification, raise your wrist to wake Apple Watch and see who's calling. Tap the Answer button on Apple Watch to talk using the microphone and speaker on Apple Watch. To scroll to answer the call using iPhone or send a text message instead, turn the Digital Crown to scroll down, then choose an option.

When you receive an incoming call, tap the green button to answer or tap the red button to send the call to voicemail.

Hold a call. Tap "Answer on iPhone" to place the call on hold until you can continue it on your paired iPhone. The caller hears a repeated sound until you pick up the call. If you can't find your iPhone, tap the ping iPhone button on Apple Watch to locate it.

Switch a call from Apple Watch to iPhone. While talking on Apple Watch, just swipe up on the Phone icon in the bottom-left corner of the iPhone Lock screen. Or, if iPhone is unlocked, tap the green bar at the top of the screen.

Adjust call volume. To adjust the speaker volume when talking on Apple Watch, turn the Digital Crown while on the call or tap the volume symbols on the screen. Tap the Mute button to mute your end of the call (if you're listening on a conference call, for example).

You can also quickly mute an incoming call by pressing the palm of your hand on the watch display and holding it there for three seconds. You must first turn on the option in the Apple Watch app on iPhone. Go to My Watch > Sounds & Haptics and turn on Cover to Mute.

Send a call to voicemail. Tap the red Decline button in the incoming call notification.

Listen to voicemail. If a caller leaves voicemail, you get a notification-- tap the Play button in the notification to listen. To listen to a voicemail later, open the Phone app phone icon, then tap Voicemail.

Make phone calls

You can ask Siri to call anyone in your Contacts.

Place a call. If the person you're calling is one of your favorites, press the side button, turn the Digital Crown or tap their initials, then tap the call button. If they're not in your friends list, open the Phone app Phone icon, then tap Favorites or Contacts. Turn the Digital Crown to scroll, then tap the name you want to call.

See call info on Apple Watch. While you're talking on iPhone, you can view call information on Apple Watch in the Phone app Phone icon. You can also end the call from Apple Watch (for example, if you're using earphones or a headset).

11. Calenders and Reminders

Check and update your calendar

The Calendar app on Apple Watch shows events you've scheduled or been invited to today and for the next week. Apple Watch shows events for all calendars you use on your iPhone.

With the Calendar app open, turn the crown to scroll events. Press the display to switch between day view and list view. Tap the date in the upper left to show a monthly calendar.

View your calendar. Open Calendar from the Home screen, or swipe up on the watch face, swipe to the Calendar glance, then tap. You can also tap today's date on your watch face if you've added the calendar to the face.

Review today's events. Open Calendar, then turn the Digital Crown to scroll. Swipe right on today's time line (Day view) to jump to the current time. To see event details, including time, location, invitee status, and notes, tap the event.

Switch between the daily time line and a single list of events. Firmly press the display while viewing a daily calendar, then tap List or Day.

View a different day. In Day view, swipe left on today's calendar to see the next day. Swipe right to go back. (You can't see any day before today, or more than seven days total.) To jump back to the current day and time, firmly press the display, then tap Today. In List view, just turn the Digital Crown.

See a full month calendar. Tap < in the upper left of any daily calendar. Tap the monthly calendar to return to Day view.

The monthly view shows the full month's calendar with today highlighted in red. Tap anywhere to return to your daily list of events.

Add or modify an event. Switch to the Calendar app on iPhone, then add the event there. If you're looking at your calendar on Apple Watch, just wake iPhone and swipe up on the Calendar icon in the lower-left corner of the Lock screen to open Calendar.

You can, for example, ask Siri to create a calendar event titled gym for April 24 at 4PM.

Display the date or an upcoming event on the watch face. You can add some combination of day and date to many of the watch faces: for example, Modular, Color, Utility, Simple, or Chronograph. The Modular, Chronograph, and Mickey Mouse faces can show the next upcoming event. Firmly press the display while viewing the watch face, swipe to a face, then tap Customize.

Respond to an invitation. If you see the invitation when it arrives, just swipe (or turn the Digital Crown to scroll) to the bottom of the notification, then tap Accept, Maybe, or Decline. If you discover the notification later, tap it in your list of notifications, then scroll and respond. If you're already in the Calendar app, just tap the event to respond.

Accept, Maybe, and Decline buttons are at the bottom of calendar invitations. Swipe or turn the crown to go to them.

Contact an event organizer. To email the event organizer, firmly press the display while you're looking at the event details. To send a voice message or call, tap the organizer's name in the event details.

Time to leave. You can schedule a "leave now" alert based on the estimated travel time to an event you create. Open the Calendar app on iPhone, tap the event, tap Edit, tap Travel Time, and turn it on. You'll get an alert that takes travel time into account.

Adjust settings. Open the Apple Watch app on iPhone, tap My Watch, then tap Calendar.

12. Health and Fitness

Track daily activity

The Activity app on Apple Watch keeps track of your movement throughout the day and helps encourage you to meet your fitness goals. The app tracks how often you stand up, how much you move, and how many minutes of exercise you do, and provides a simple and powerful graphic ring of your daily activity. The goal is to sit less, move more, and get some exercise by completing each ring every day. The Activity app on iPhone keeps a long-term record of all your activity.

Get started. The first time you open the Activity app on Apple Watch, swipe left to read the Move, Exercise, and Stand descriptions, then tap Get Started. Enter the required information by tapping Sex, Age, Weight, and Height, then turn the Digital Crown to set and tap Continue. Finally, tap Start Moving.

In the Activity app, you can set 3 daily fitness goals: Stand, Move, and Exercise.
Note: You can also enter your birthdate, sex, height, and weight in the Apple Watch app on iPhone. In the Apple Watch app, tap My Watch, then tap Health.

Check your progress. Swipe up on the watch face, then swipe to the Activity glance at any time to see how you're doing. Tap the glance to open the Activity app icon and swipe to see the individual activities. The Move ring shows how many active calories you've burned. The Exercise ring shows how many minutes of brisk activity you've done. The Stand ring shows how many times in the day you've stood for at least one minute per hour. Swipe up on an activity or turn the Digital Crown to see your progress as a graph.

Workout progress shown as a ring or a graph in the Activity glance. An overlapping ring means you've exceeded your goal. Watch for achievement awards, if you have that feature turned on.In the

Activity glance, colored rings mark your progress toward your Move, Exercise, and Stand daily goals.

Check your activity history and see all your achievements. Open the Activity app on iPhone, then tap a date in the calendar to see a breakdown for that day. You'll see how many steps you took and the distance you covered, in addition to Move, Exercise, and Stand info.

Adjust your goals. Open Activity icon on Apple Watch and firmly press the display until you see the prompt to change your Move goal.

In the Activity app, press the screen to change your daily Move goal. Every Monday, you'll also be notified about the previous week's achievements, and you can adjust your daily Move goal for the coming week. Apple Watch suggests goals based on your previous performance.

Control activity notifications. Reminders can help when it comes to meeting goals. Apple Watch can let you know if you're on track or falling behind your activity goals. It can even alert you if you've been sitting too long. To choose which reminders and alerts you'd like to see, open the Apple Watch app on iPhone, tap My Watch, then tap Activity.

Activity screen in Apple Watch app, where you can customize the notifications you want to get and whether you want to show the Activity glance.

Monitor your workouts

The Workout app on Apple Watch gives you tools to manage your individual workout sessions. It lets you set specific goals, such as time, distance, or calories, then tracks your progress, nudges you along the way, and summarizes your results. You can use the Activity app on iPhone to review your complete workout history. See Keep your data accurate for information on how Apple Watch is calibrated.

Start a workout. Open the Workout icon, then tap the workout type you're going for. As you use the app and choose workouts, the order of workouts will reflect your preferences.

In the Workout app, tap to select a workout and turn the Digital Crown to see the list of workouts.
On the goal screen, swipe left and right to choose a calorie, time, or distance goal (or no goal), then turn the Digital Crown or tap + / – to set. When you're ready to go, tap Start. If you're measuring calories or time, you can leave iPhone behind and exercise with just Apple Watch. But for the most accurate distance measurements outdoors, take iPhone along.

You can set your time, distance, or calorie goals by tapping the plus and minus buttons.

Note: Outdoor and Indoor Walk/Run/Cycle are distinct workouts because Apple Watch calculates the calorie burn differently for each. For indoor workouts, Apple Watch relies mainly on your heart rate readings for calorie estimates, but for outdoor workouts, Apple Watch works in conjunction with iPhone (which has GPS) to calculate speed and distance. Those values, along with your heart rate, are used to estimate the number of calories burned.

Check your progress. Check the completion ring during your workout for a quick indication of your progress. Swipe on the lower half of the screen to review elapsed time, average pace, distance covered, calories consumed, and heart rate. Instead of viewing the progress rings, you can choose to see your distance, calorie, or time values numerically. Open the Apple Watch app on iPhone, tap My Watch, then turn on Workout > Show Goal Metric.

During a workout, you can swipe the screen to see your progress--or take your heart rate.
Pause and resume. To pause the workout at any time, firmly press the display, then tap Pause. To continue, firmly press the display again, then tap Resume.

Conserve power during a long workout. You can save power by disabling the heart rate sensor during long walking and running workouts. Your calorie burn estimates might not be as accurate. Open the Apple Watch app on iPhone, tap My Watch, then turn on Workout > Power Saving Mode.

End the workout. When you reach your goal, you'll hear an alarm. If you're feeling good and want to continue, go ahead—Apple Watch continues to collect data until you tell it to stop. When you're ready, firmly press the display, then tap End. Turn the Digital Crown to scroll through the results summary, then tap Save or Discard at the bottom.

Review your workout history. Open the Activity app on iPhone, then tap a date. Scroll down to see your workouts listed below the Move/Stand/Exercise summaries. Swipe left on a workout to see details for it.

Check your heart rate

For best results, the back of Apple Watch needs skin contact for features like wrist detection, haptic notifications, and the heart rate sensor. Wearing Apple Watch with the right fit-- not too tight, not too loose, and with room for your skin to breathe-- will keep you comfortable and let the sensors do their job. You may want to tighten Apple Watch for workouts, then loosen the band when you're done. In addition, the sensors will work only when you wear Apple Watch on the top of your wrist.

See your current heart rate. Swipe up on the watch face, then swipe to the Heartbeat glance to measure your heart rate and see your last reading. Tap the heart in the glance to take a new reading.

Swipe to the Heartbeat glance and tap the heart icon to get your heart rate.
Check your heart rate during a workout. Swipe on the lower half of the Workout icon progress screen.

During a workout, you can swipe the bottom of the screen to check your heart rate.

Keep your data accurate

Apple Watch uses the information you provide about your height, weight, gender, and age to calculate how many calories you burn, how far you travel, and other data. In addition, the more you run with the Workout app, the more Apple Watch learns your fitness level-- and the more accurately it can estimate the calories you've burned during aerobic activity.

Your iPhone GPS allows Apple Watch to achieve even more distance accuracy. For example, if you carry iPhone while using the Workout app-- on a run, Apple Watch uses the iPhone GPS to calibrate your stride. Then later, if you're not carrying iPhone, or if you're working out where GPS is unavailable (for example, indoors), Apple Watch uses the stored information about your stride to measure distance.

Update your height and weight. Open the Apple Watch app on iPhone, tap My Watch, tap Health, Weight, or Height, and adjust.

13. Apple Pay and Passbook

Make purchases with Apple Pay

You can use Apple Pay on Apple Watch to make purchases in stores that accept contactless payments. Just set up Apple Pay in the Apple Watch app on iPhone, and you're ready to make purchases-- even if you don't have iPhone with you.

If you unpair Apple Watch, disable your passcode, or turn off wrist detection, you can't use Apple Pay.

You can add up to eight credit or debit cards; they'll appear at the top of the stack in your Passbook app, above your passes. The last four or five digits of your credit or debit card number appear on the front of a payment card.

Note: Many U.S. credit and debit cards can be used with Apple Pay.

The Passbook screen on Apple Watch shows payment cards first, with passes below.
Set up Apple Pay on Apple Watch. Even if you've already set up Apple Pay on iPhone using the Passbook app, you need to add the credit or debit cards to use on Apple Watch. Have your credit or debit card handy, then open the Apple Watch app on iPhone. Tap My Watch, tap Passbook & Apple Pay, tap Add Credit or Debit Card, then tap Next. If you have a supported credit or debit card on file with iTunes or the App Store, enter the card's security code. Otherwise, use the iPhone camera to capture the information on your credit or debit card, then fill in any additional information needed, including the card security code. Note that your card issuer may require additional steps to verify your identity. If so, choose a verification option, tap Verify, then tap Enter Code to complete verification.

Passbook & Apple Pay settings screen in the Apple Watch app.
Pointer to the word Verify, tap to enter the verification code for your

payment card. Tap Add Credit or Debit Card to add a new payment card.

Add another credit or debit card. In the Apple Watch app on iPhone, tap My Watch, tap Passbook & Apple Pay, tap Add Credit or Debit Card, then follow the on screen instructions.

Choose your default card. In the Apple Watch app on iPhone, tap My Watch, tap Passbook & Apple Pay, tap Default Card, then select the desired card.

Pay for a purchase. Double-click the side button, swipe to change cards, then hold Apple Watch within a few centimeters of the contactless card reader, with the display facing the reader. A gentle pulse and tone confirm the payment information was sent.

Find the Device Account Number for a card. When you make a payment with Apple Watch, the Device Account Number of the card is sent with the payment to the merchant. To find the last four or five digits of this number, open the Apple Watch app on iPhone, tap My Watch, tap Passbook & Apple Pay, then tap a card.

Remove a card from Apple Pay. Open Passbook on Apple Watch, tap to select a card, firmly press the card, then tap Delete. Or open the Apple Watch app on iPhone, tap My Watch, tap Passbook & Apple Pay, tap the card, then tap Remove.

If Apple Watch is lost or stolen. If your Apple Watch is lost or stolen, sign in to your account at iCloud.com and remove your cards. Go to Settings > My Devices, choose the device, and click Remove All. You can also call the issuers of your cards.

Use Passbook

Use the Passbook app on Apple Watch to keep your boarding passes, movie tickets, loyalty cards, and more all in one place. Your passes in Passbook on iPhone automatically sync to Apple Watch (if you've turned on Mirror iPhone in the Apple Watch app). Scan a pass on Apple Watch to check in for a flight, get into a movie, or redeem a coupon. To set options for your passes on Apple Watch, open the

Apple Watch app on iPhone, tap My Watch, then tap Passbook & Apple Pay.

Use a pass. If a notification for a pass appears on Apple Watch, tap the notification to display the pass. You might have to scroll to get to the barcode. Or open Passbook, select the pass, then present the barcode on the pass to the scanner.

Rearrange passes. On iPhone, open the Passbook app, and drag to rearrange passes. The order will be reflected on Apple Watch.

Done with a pass? Delete the pass on iPhone. Open the Passbook app, tap the pass, tap the Info button, then tap Delete.

14. Maps and Directions

Exploring the Map

Apple Watch has a Maps glance for a quick look at your location and surroundings, and a full Maps app for exploring and getting directions.

You can ask Siri to show Berlin on the map.

See a map. Open the Maps app on Apple Watch. Or, for a quick look at your location, swipe up on your watch face, then swipe to the Maps glance. Tap the Maps glance to open the full Maps app.

Tap the Tracking button in the lower left corner of the map to see your location, indicated by a blue dot.

Pan and zoom. To pan the map, drag with one finger. To zoom in or out, turn the Digital Crown. You can also double-tap the map to zoom in on the spot you tap. Tap the Tracking button in the lower left to get back to your current location.

Search the map. While viewing the map, firmly press the display, tap Search, then tap Dictate or tap a location in the list of places you've explored recently.

Get info about a landmark or location. Tap the location on the map, then turn the Digital Crown to scroll the information. Tap < in the upper left to return to the map.

Stick a pin. Touch and hold the map where you want the pin to go, wait for the pin to drop, then let go. Now you can tap the pin for address information, or use it as the starting point or destination for directions. To move the pin, just drop a new one in the new location.

Use a map pin to get the approximate address of a spot on the map, or use it as a starting point or destination for directions.

Find the approximate address of any spot on the map. Drop a pin on the location, then tap the pin to see address info.

Call a location. Tap the phone number in the location info. To switch to iPhone, swipe up on the Phone icon in the lower-left corner of the Lock screen, then tap the green bar at the top of the screen.

See a contact's address on the map. While viewing the map, firmly press the display, tap Contacts, turn the Digital Crown to scroll, then tap the contact.

See your current location and surroundings. Open Maps icon, then tap the current location arrow in the lower left. Or swipe to the Maps glance, which always shows where you are. If you have an upcoming calendar event, the Maps glance shows directions to it.

Get Directions

Get directions to a landmark or map pin. Open Maps, then tap the destination landmark or map pin. Scroll the location information until you see Directions, then tap Walking or Driving. When you're ready to go, tap Start, then follow the directions.

Get directions to a search result or contact. While viewing the map, firmly press the display, then tap Search or Contacts.

Ask Siri for directions. Just tell Siri where you'd like to go.

Follow directions. After you tap Start and head off on your first leg, Apple Watch uses taps to let you know when to turn. A steady series of 12 taps means turn right at the intersection you're approaching; three pairs of two taps means turn left. Not sure what your destination looks like? You'll feel a vibration when you're on the last leg, and again when you arrive.

Check your progress. Swipe left on the current step of the directions, or tap the dots at the bottom of the screen to see a map view.

While you're following directions, your estimated time of arrival is in the upper left. Press the screen at any time to cancel the directions.

Find out when you'll get there. Look in the upper-left corner for your estimated time of arrival. Current time is in the upper right.

End directions before you get there. Firmly press the display, then tap Stop Directions.

15. Music Mastery

Play music on iPhone

You can use the Music app or the Now Playing glance on Apple Watch to control music playback on iPhone.

You can ask Siri to play a song by title.

Play music on iPhone. Open the Music icon on Apple Watch. Browse through playlists, albums, artists, or songs until you see a list of songs, then tap a song to play it.

If you don't see the music you're expecting, make sure iPhone, not Apple Watch, is your source-- firmly press the display, tap Source, then tap iPhone.

When playing music, tap Back button in the upper left to return to the track list. Previous Track, Play/Pause, and Next Track buttons are in the center of the screen. Turn the crown to adjust volume. Press the screen to shuffle or repeat songs, or to switch to playing songs on Apple Watch instead of iPhone.

See album art for the current song. Tap the album name above the playback controls. Tap again to return to the controls.

Send audio to another device with AirPlay. While viewing the playback controls, firmly press the display, tap AirPlay, then choose a destination.

Shuffle or repeat songs. While viewing the playback controls, firmly press the display, then tap Shuffle or Repeat.

Control playback with the glance. Use the Now Playing glance for quick control. Swipe up on the watch face, then swipe to the playback controls.

If you don't see the Now Playing glance, open the Apple Watch app on iPhone, tap My Watch, then turn on Music > Show in Glances.

Play music on Apple Watch

You can store music right on Apple Watch, then listen to it on Bluetooth headphones or speakers without your iPhone nearby.

Store songs on Apple Watch. Open the Apple Watch app on iPhone, tap My Watch, go to Music > Synced Playlist, then choose the playlist of songs you want to move to Apple Watch. Then, place Apple Watch on its charger to complete the sync.

When the music has been synced, open the Settings app Settings icon on Apple Watch, go to General > About, and look under Songs to see the number of songs copied.

You can use the Music app on iPhone to create a playlist specifically for music you want to listen to on Apple Watch.

Pair Bluetooth headphones or speakers. Follow the instructions that came with the headphones or speakers to put them in discovery mode. When the Bluetooth device is ready, open the Settings app on Apple Watch, tap Bluetooth, then tap the device when it appears.

If you switch the music source to Apple Watch before you pair Bluetooth speakers or headphones, a Settings button appears in the center of the screen that takes you to Bluethooth settings on Apple Watch, where you can add a listening device.

Play songs stored on Apple Watch. Open Music Music icon on Apple Watch, firmly press the display, tap Source, then choose Watch.

Control playback. Swipe to the Now Playing glance for quick control. Swipe up on the watch face, then swipe to the playback controls. You can also control playback using the Music app Music icon.

Limit the songs stored on Apple Watch. Open the Apple Watch app on iPhone, tap My Watch, go to Music > Playlist Limit, then choose a storage limit or maximum number of songs to be stored on Apple Watch.

See how much music is stored on Apple Watch. On Apple Watch, open the Settings app Settings icon, go to General > About, and look under Songs.

16. Remote Control

Control music on a Mac or PC

You can use the Remote app on Apple Watch to play music in iTunes on a computer on the same Wi-Fi network.

Add an iTunes library. Open the Remote icon on Apple Watch, then tap Add Device +. In iTunes on your computer, click the Remote button near the top of the iTunes window, then enter the 4-digit code displayed on Apple Watch.

Don't look for the Remote button in iTunes before you tap Add Device on Apple Watch-- the button appears only when a remote is trying to connect. In iTunes 12 and later, the Remote button is in the upper left, below the Volume slider. In iTunes 11 and earlier, the Remote button is in the upper right, below the Search field.

The Remote button in iTunes appears while you're trying to add the library to Apple Watch.

Choose a library to play from. If you have only one library, you should be good to go. If you've added more than one library, tap the one you want when you open Remote on Apple Watch. If you're already playing music, tap the Back button in the upper left of the playback controls, then tap the library.

Control playback. Use the playback controls in the Remote app.

Remove a library. In the Remote app on Apple Watch, tap the Back button in the upper left to view your devices, firmly press the display, then tap Edit. When the device icons jiggle, tap x on the one you want to remove, then tap Remove. If that was your only remote device, you're finished-- otherwise, tap the checkmark to finish editing.

Control Apple TV

You can use Apple Watch as a remote control for your Apple TV when you're connected to the same Wi-Fi network.

Pair Apple Watch with Apple TV. If your iPhone has never joined the Wi-Fi network that Apple TV is on, join it now. Then, open the Remote app icon on Apple Watch and tap Add Device +. On your Apple TV, go to Settings > General > Remotes, select your Apple Watch, then enter the passcode displayed on Apple Watch.

When the pairing icon appears next to Apple Watch, it's ready to control Apple TV.

Control Apple TV. Make sure Apple TV is awake. Open the Remote app icon on Apple Watch, choose Apple TV, then swipe up, down, left, or right to move through Apple TV menu options. Tap to choose the selected item. Tap the Menu button to go back, or touch and hold it to return to the top menu. Tap the Play/Pause button to pause or resume playback.

The Apple Watch display becomes a remote control when connected to an Apple TV. Swipe anywhere on the screen to change the Apple TV selection. The Menu button is in the lower left and the Play/Pause button is in the lower right. When you're finished, tap the Back button in the upper left.

Unpair and remove Apple TV. On your Apple TV, go to Settings > General > Remotes, then select your Apple Watch under iOS Remotes to remove it. Then, open the Remote app icon on Apple Watch and, when the "lost connection" message appears, tap Remove.

17. Photo Gallery

View photos on Apple Watch

Photos from the iPhone album of your choice are stored on Apple Watch, and appear in the Photos app on Apple Watch. When you first get Apple Watch, it's set to use your Favorites album-- photos you've tagged as favorites-- but you can change the album it uses.

In the Photos app, tap any photo in the collection to view it. Turn the crown to zoom out from a particular photo to view the collection.

Browse photos on Apple Watch. Open the Photos app on Apple Watch, then tap a photo. Swipe left or right to see others. Turn the Digital Crown to zoom or drag to pan. Zoom all the way out to see the entire album.

While viewing a photo, turn the crown to zoom, drag to pan, or double-tap to switch between viewing all of the photo and filling the screen. Swipe left or right to see the next photo.

18. Camera Remote

Use remote viewfinder and shutter

If you want to position iPhone for a photo and then not touch it, or if you can't see the iPhone display to frame a shot, you can use Apple Watch to view the iPhone camera image and tap the shutter.

To function as a camera remote, Apple Watch needs to be within normal Bluetooth range of iPhone (about 33 feet or 10 meters).

When looking at the camera Remote viewfinder on Apple Watch, the Take Picture button is bottom center with the Take Picture After Delay button to its right. If you've taken a photo, the Photo Viewer button is in the lower left.
Take a photo. Open the Camera app Camera Remote icon, then position iPhone to frame the shot using Apple Watch as your viewfinder. To adjust exposure, tap the key area of the shot in the preview on Apple Watch. To take the shot, tap the Shutter button.

The photo is captured in Photos on your iPhone, but you can review it on Apple Watch.

Review your shots. Tap the thumbnail in the lower left. Swipe right or left to see other shots. While viewing a shot, turn the Digital Crown to zoom. To pan, drag with your finger. Tap anywhere to hide or show the Close button and the shot count. Double-tap to fill the screen or see the whole shot. When you're finished, tap Close.

Use the shutter timer

You can use Apple Watch to set a shutter timer for a group shot without having to sprint back into the frame.

Use the shutter timer. Open the Camera app Camera Remote icon, then tap the Timer button in the lower right. A beep, a tap, and flashes from iPhone let you know when to expect the shot.

When looking at the camera Remote viewfinder on Apple Watch, the Timer button is in the bottom right.

The timer takes a burst of shots, so you're sure to get a good one. To pick the best shot, view the photo in Photos on iPhone, then tap Select (below the photo).

19. Stocks

Track stocks

Use the Stocks app on Apple Watch to see info on the stocks you follow on your iPhone.

You can ask Siri for the closing price of a stock.

Follow the market. To browse your stocks, open the Stocks app icon on Apple Watch.

See details about a stock. Tap it in the list, then turn the Digital Crown to scroll. Tap the performance graph (or the time indicators below it) to change the time scale. Tap < in the upper left to return to the stocks list.

Information about a stock in the Stocks app. Turn the Digital Crown to see more details.
Add, delete, or reorder stocks. Add, delete, or change the order of stocks using the Stocks app on iPhone. Changes you make there are reflected on Apple Watch.

Choose the data you see. Open the Stocks app on iPhone, then tap the Points Change for any stock to see Percentage Change or Market Cap.

Switch to Stocks on iPhone. While looking at the Stocks app stocks icon or Stocks glance on Apple Watch, swipe up on the Stocks icon in the lower-left corner of the iPhone Lock screen.

Check one stock at a Glance

Use the Stocks glance to check one stock of particular interest.

View the Stocks glance. Swipe up on the watch face, then swipe to the stock info.

Tap the Stocks glance to open the Stock app.
If you don't see the Stocks glance, open the Apple Watch app on iPhone, then go to My Watch > Glances and add it to your list of glances.

Choose your stock. Open the Apple Watch app on iPhone, tap My Watch, tap Stocks, then choose your default stock.

You can set your default stock to mirror your iPhone, or to another stock of your choice.

Add stock info to your watch face

You can add stock info to these faces:

Modular (ticker name and price)

Utility (ticker name, price, and change)

Mickey Mouse (ticker name, price, and change)

Add stock info to a watch face. While viewing the face, firmly press the display, then tap Customize. Swipe left until you can select individual face features, tap the one you'd like to use, then turn the Digital Crown to choose Stocks. When you're finished, press the Digital Crown.

Choose the stock shown on the watch face. Open the Apple Watch app on iPhone, tap My Watch, tap Stocks, then choose a default stock. If you choose Mirror iPhone, the stock shown on the watch face is the last one you highlighted in the Stocks app on iPhone.

Choose the data you see on the watch face. Open the Apple Watch app on iPhone, tap My Watch, tap Stocks, then tap Current Price, Points Change, Percentage Change, or Market Cap.

20. Weather

Check the weather

Check current conditions. For current temperature plus a summary of current conditions and the high and low temperatures for the day, check the Weather glance.

See more details and forecasts. For current temperature and conditions, hourly forecasts of temperature, conditions, and precipitation, and a 10-day forecast, open the Weather app weather icon on Apple Watch and tap a city. Tap the Hourly Conditions display repeatedly to switch to hourly precipitation or hourly temperature forecasts. Scroll down to see a 10-day forecast.

In the Weather app, tap the current temperature to switch to an hourly temperature or precipitation forecast. Scroll down to see a 10-day forecast. Swipe left or right to see conditions in other cities. Add a city. Open the Weather app on iPhone, then tap the + at the bottom of the list of cities, and select a city. The Weather app on Apple Watch shows the same cities, in the same order, that you add to the Weather app on iPhone.

Choose your default city. Open the Apple Watch app on iPhone, tap My Watch, then go to Weather > Default City. Conditions for that city are shown in the Weather glance and on the watch face, if you've added weather to the face.

See weather on your watch face

You can include weather info on these watch faces:

Utility (temperature, or temperature and conditions)

Modular (temperature, or temperature, conditions, high, and low)

Simple (temperature)

Color (temperature)

Chronograph (temperature)

Mickey Mouse (temperature, or temperature and conditions)

Add weather to your watch face. While viewing the face, firmly press the display, then tap Customize. Swipe left until you can select individual face features, tap the one where you'd like to see weather info, then turn the Digital Crown to choose Weather. When you're finished, press the Digital Crown.

Tap the temperature on a watch face to open the Weather app. Choose the city for the watch face weather. Open the Apple Watch app on iPhone, tap My Watch, then go to Weather > Default City.

Open the full Weather app. Tap the temperature on the watch face.

21. Accessibility

VoiceOver

VoiceOver helps you use Apple Watch even if you can't see the display. Use simple gestures to move around the screen and listen as VoiceOver speaks each item you select.

Turn on VoiceOver. On Apple Watch, open the Settings icon, then turn on General > Accessibility > VoiceOver. You can also use iPhone to turn on VoiceOver for Apple Watch-- open the Apple Watch app on iPhone, tap My Watch, then tap the VoiceOver option in General > Accessibility. Or, use the Accessibility Shortcut. See The Accessibility Shortcut. And there's always Siri:

You can ask Siri to turn VoiceOver on.

Explore the screen. Move your finger around on the display and listen as the name of each item you touch is spoken. You can also tap with one finger to select an item, or swipe left or right with one finger to select an adjacent item. Swipe left or right, up or down with two fingers to see other pages. (For example, swipe up with two fingers on the watch face to see glances, then swipe left or right with two fingers to see the different glances.)

Go back. Gone down a path you didn't expect? Do a two-finger scrub: use two fingers to trace a "z" shape on the display.

Act on an item. With VoiceOver on, use a double tap instead of a single tap to open an app, switch an option, or perform any action that would normally be done with a tap. Select an app icon or option switch by tapping it or swiping to it, then double-tap to perform its action. For example, to turn VoiceOver off, select the VoiceOver button, then double-tap anywhere on the display.

Perform additional actions. Some items offer several actions-- listen for "actions available" when you select an item. Swipe up or down to choose an action, then double-tap to perform it. (For example, when you select the watch face, you can swipe up or down to choose from go-to-glances and go-to-notification-center actions.)

Pause reading. To have VoiceOver stop reading, tap the display with two fingers. Tap again with two fingers to resume.

Adjust VoiceOver volume. Double-tap and hold with two fingers, then slide up or down. Or, open the Apple Watch app on iPhone, tap My Watch, then go to General > Accessibility > VoiceOver and drag the slider.

Adjust reading rate. Open the Apple Watch app on iPhone, tap My Watch, then go to General > Accessibility > VoiceOver and drag the sliders.

Turn off the display. For privacy, turn on the screen curtain so no one can see what's on Apple Watch while you use VoiceOver. Open the Settings app Settings icon on Apple Watch, then turn on General > Accessibility > VoiceOver > Screen Curtain.

Turn off VoiceOver. Open the Settings app Settings icon, go to General > Accessibility > VoiceOver, then tap the VoiceOver button.

You can also ask Siri to turn VoiceOver off.

VoiceOver for Setup. VoiceOver can help you set up your Apple Watch-- triple-press the Digital Crown during setup.

Set up Apple Watch using VoiceOver

VoiceOver can help you set up Apple Watch and pair it with your iPhone. To highlight a button or other item, swipe left or right on the display with one finger. Tap to activate the highlighted item.

Set up Apple Watch using VoiceOver
If Apple Watch isn't on, turn it on by holding down the side button (below the Digital Crown).

On Apple Watch, turn on VoiceOver by triple-clicking the Digital Crown.

Swipe right or left on the display to choose a language, then double-tap to select it.

Swipe right to highlight the Start Pairing button, then double-tap.

On iPhone, turn on VoiceOver by going to Settings > General > Accessibility > VoiceOver.

To open the Apple Watch app, go to the iPhone Home screen, swipe right to select the Apple Watch app, then double-tap.

To get iPhone ready to pair, swipe right to select the Start Pairing button, then double-tap.

The "Hold Apple Watch up to the Camera" screen appears.

To try automatic pairing, point the iPhone camera at the watch from about 6 inches away.

When you hear the pairing confirmation, you can skip to step 14. If you have difficulty, you can try manual pairing, steps 9 through 13.

Swipe right to select the Pair Apple Watch Manually button, then double-tap.

On Apple Watch, find your Apple Watch ID: swipe right to the Info About Pairing Apple Watch Manually button, then double-tap. Swipe right once to hear the unique identifier for your Apple Watch—it'll be something like "Apple Watch 52345".

On iPhone, select your Apple Watch: swipe right until you hear the same Apple Watch identifier that was just displayed on Apple Watch, then double-tap.

To get your pairing code, on Apple Watch, swipe right until you hear the six-digit pairing code.

Enter the pairing code from Apple Watch on iPhone using the keyboard.

When pairing succeeds, you hear "Your Apple Watch is paired." If pairing fails, tap to respond to the alerts, then Apple Watch and the Apple Watch app on iPhone reset so you can try again.

When pairing is complete, on iPhone, swipe right to the Set Up Apple Watch button, then double-tap.

To choose your wrist preference, swipe right on the Wrist Preference screen to select Left or Right, then double-tap.

Review the terms and conditions, swipe right on the Terms and Conditions screen to select Agree, then double-tap. Select and double-tap Agree in the alert that appears.

To enter the password for your Apple ID, swipe right to the Enter Password button, double-tap, then enter the password for the Apple ID you use on your iPhone. Then double-tap the Return key in the lower-right corner of the keyboard.

To choose a Location Services option, swipe to your choice, then double-tap.

To choose a Siri option, swipe to your choice, then double-tap.

To create an Apple Watch passcode, swipe right on the Passcode screen to select Create a Passcode, then double-tap. On Apple Watch, enter a four-digit passcode of your choice, then reenter to confirm. Swipe, tap, or drag your finger around the display to select a number, then double-tap.

On Apple Watch, choose whether to unlock Apple Watch when you unlock iPhone.

To choose whether to install additional apps on Apple Watch, swipe to highlight Install All or Choose Later on iPhone, then double-tap.

Zoom

Use Zoom to magnify what's on the Apple Watch display.

Turn on Zoom. On Apple Watch, open the Settings app icon, then turn on General > Accessibility > Zoom. You can also use iPhone to turn on Zoom for Apple Watch-- open the Apple Watch app on iPhone, tap My Watch, tap Settings, then tap the option in General > Accessibility. Or, use the Accessibility Shortcut; see The Accessibility Shortcut.

Zoom in or out. Double-tap the Apple Watch display with two fingers.

Move around (pan). Drag the display with two fingers. You can also turn the Digital Crown to pan over the entire page, left-right and up-down. The small Zoom button that appears shows you where you are on the page.

Use the Digital Crown normally instead of panning. Tap the display once with two fingers to switch between using the Digital Crown to pan and using the Digital Crown the way it works without Zoom on (for example, to scroll a list or zoom a map).

Adjust magnification. Double-tap and hold with two fingers, then drag the fingers up or down on the display. To limit magnification, open the Apple Watch app on iPhone, tap My Watch, go to General > Accessibility > Zoom, then drag the Maximum Zoom Level slider.

Zoom during setup. Triple-tap with two fingers while setting up Apple Watch to get a better look.

22. Safety and Support

Restart Apple Watch

If something isn't working right, try restarting or resetting Apple Watch and its paired iPhone.

Restart Apple Watch. To turn off Apple Watch, press and hold the side button until the sliders appear, then drag the Power Off slider to the right. To turn Apple Watch back on, hold down the side button until the Apple logo appears.

Restart the paired iPhone. To turn off iPhone, press and hold the Sleep/Wake button until the slider appears, then drag the slider to the right. To turn iPhone back on, hold down the Sleep/Wake button until the Apple logo appears.

If you can't turn off Apple Watch or if the problem continues, you may need to force Apple Watch to restart. Do this only if you're unable to restart your Apple Watch.

Force Apple Watch to restart. Hold down the side button and the Digital Crown at the same time for at least ten seconds, until the Apple logo appears.

Restore Apple Watch

If Apple Watch is disabled because you forgot your passcode or entered an incorrect passcode too many times, you can use the Apple Watch app on iPhone to allow you to enter the passcode again. If you still can't remember your passcode, you can restore Apple Watch and reset the passcode. Restoring erases the content and settings on Apple Watch, but uses a backup to replace your data and settings. For more information, see Update Apple Watch software.

Important: If Erase Data is turned on, the data on your Apple Watch is erased after 10 failed passcode attempts.

Update Apple Watch software

You can update your Apple Watch software by checking for updates in the Apple Watch app on iPhone.

Check for software updates. Open the Apple Watch app on iPhone, tap My Watch, then go to General > Software Update. Download the software to the iPhone, then continue on Apple Watch.

Update wirelessly on Apple Watch. Follow the prompts on Apple Watch to install the software update (or restore your software, if necessary).

Restore Apple Watch from a backup

Apple Watch content backs up automatically to your paired iPhone, and you can restore it from a stored backup. Apple Watch backups are included as part of your iPhone backups to iCloud or iTunes, but you can't view information in the backups in iCloud.

Backing up and restoring Apple Watch. When paired with an iPhone, Apple Watch content is backed up continuously to iPhone. If you unpair the devices, a backup is performed first. If you repair Apple Watch or get a new one, you can choose Restore from Backup and select a stored backup on your iPhone.

Remove, change, and fasten bands

Follow these general instructions for removing, changing, and fastening bands, and then find the instructions for your specific band later in this section. Make sure you're replacing a band with one of the same size. The bands are sized according to the size of Apple Watch and should not be used interchangeably. Some band styles are made for a particular size Apple Watch only.

Change bands. Press the band release button on Apple Watch, slide the band across to remove it, then slide the new band in. Never force a band into the slot. If you're having trouble removing or inserting a band, press the band release button again.

For best results, the back of Apple Watch needs skin contact for features like wrist detection, haptic notifications, and the heart rate sensor. Wearing Apple Watch with the right fit-- not too tight, not too loose, and with room for your skin to breathe-- will keep you comfortable and let the sensors do their job. You may want to tighten Apple Watch for workouts, then loosen the band when you're done. In addition, the sensors will work only when you wear Apple Watch on the top of your wrist.

Important handling information

Exposure to liquid Apple Watch is water resistant but not waterproof. You may, for example, wear and use Apple Watch during exercise (exposure to sweat is OK), in the rain, and while washing your hands. If water splashes on to the watch, wipe it off with a nonabrasive, lint-free cloth. Try to minimize exposing Apple Watch to these substances and follow the instructions below in the "Cleaning and care" section if Apple Watch comes into contact with them:

Soap, detergent, acids or acidic foods, and any liquids other than fresh water, such as salt water, soapy water, pool water, perfume, insect repellent, lotions, sunscreen, oil, adhesive remover, hair dye, or solvents.

Submerging Apple Watch is not recommended. The leather bands are not water resistant. Water resistance is not a permanent condition and Apple Watch cannot be rechecked or resealed for water resistance. The following may affect the water resistance of Apple Watch and should be avoided:

Dropping Apple Watch or subjecting it to other impacts.

Submerging Apple Watch in water for long periods of time.

Swimming or bathing with Apple Watch.

Exposing Apple Watch to pressurized water or high velocity water, for example, showering, water skiing, wake boarding, surfing, jet skiing, and so on.

Wearing Apple Watch in the sauna or steam room.

Cleaning and care Keep Apple Watch clean and dry. Clean and dry Apple Watch, the band, and your skin after workouts or heavy sweating. Dry Apple Watch and the band thoroughly if they are exposed to fresh water. Clean Apple Watch if it comes in contact with anything that may cause stains, or other damage, such as dirt or sand, makeup, ink, soap, detergent, acids or acidic foods, or comes in contact with liquids other than fresh water, including those that may lead to skin irritation such as: sweat, salt water, soapy water, pool water, perfume, insect repellent, lotions, sunscreen, oil, adhesive remover, hair dye, or solvents. The Apple Watch and band colors may vary or fade over time.

How to clean Apple Watch:

Turn off Apple Watch. Press and hold the side button, then drag the Power Off slider to the right.

Depress the band release buttons and remove the band. See Remove, change, and fasten bands.

Wipe Apple Watch clean with a nonabrasive, lint-free cloth. If necessary, you can also lightly dampen the cloth with fresh water.

Dry Apple Watch with a nonabrasive, lint-free cloth.

Apple Watch Edition (gold) models benefit the most if you clean them regularly. Clean with a nonabrasive, lint-free cloth to remove surface oil, perfumes, lotions, and other substances, especially before storing Apple Watch Edition.

The following things are not recommended in the care of your Apple Watch:

Don't clean Apple Watch while it's charging.

Don't dry Apple Watch or the bands using any external heat source (for example, a hair dryer).

Don't use cleaning products or compressed air when cleaning your Apple Watch.

The front of Apple Watch is made of Ion-X glass (strengthened glass) or sapphire crystal, each with a fingerprint-resistant oleophobic (oil repellent) coating. This coating wears over time with normal usage. Cleaning products and abrasive materials will further diminish the coating, and may scratch the glass or the sapphire crystal.

Using buttons, Digital Crown, connectors, and ports Never apply excessive pressure to a button or the Digital Crown on Apple Watch, or force a charging connector into a port, because this may cause damage that is not covered under the warranty. If the connector and port don't join with reasonable ease, they probably don't match. Check for obstructions and make sure that the connector matches the port and that you have positioned the connector correctly in relation to the port.

Certain usage patterns can contribute to the fraying or breaking of cables. The cable attached to a charging unit, like any other metal wire or cable, is subject to becoming weak or brittle if repeatedly bent in the same spot. Aim for gentle curves instead of angles in the cable. Regularly inspect the cable and connector for any kinks, breaks, bends, or other damage. Should you find any such damage, discontinue use of the cable.

Lightning to USB Cable Discoloration of the Lightning connector after regular use is normal. Dirt, debris, and exposure to moisture may cause discoloration. If your Lightning cable or connector become warm during use or if Apple Watch won't charge or sync, disconnect the cable from the power adapter and clean the Lightning connector with a nonabrasive, dry, lint-free cloth. Do not use liquids or cleaning products when cleaning the Lightning connector.

Magnetic Charging Cable and Magnetic Charging Case
Discoloration of the charging surface of the Apple Watch Magnetic Charging Cable and the Apple Watch Magnetic Charging Case may occur after regular use due to dirt and debris that come in contact with the magnetic surface. This is normal. Cleaning the magnetic charging surface may reduce, or prevent, such discoloration, and will help to prevent damage to your charger and Apple Watch. To clean the charging surface, disconnect the charger from both Apple Watch and the power adapter and wipe with a damp, nonabrasive cloth. Dry with a nonabrasive, lint-free cloth before resuming charging. Do not use cleaning products when cleaning the charging surface.

Operating temperature Apple Watch is designed to work best in ambient temperatures between 32° and 95° F (0° and 35° C) and be stored in temperatures between -4° and 113° F (-20° and 45° C). Apple Watch can be damaged and battery life shortened if stored or operated outside of these temperature ranges. Avoid exposing Apple Watch to dramatic changes in temperature or humidity. If the interior temperature of Apple Watch exceeds normal operating temperatures (for example, in a hot car or in direct sunlight for extended periods of time), you may experience the following as it attempts to regulate its temperature:

Charging may slow or stop.

The display may dim.

A temperature warning screen may appear.

Some data transfer may be paused or delayed.

Some apps may close.

Important: You may not be able to use Apple Watch while the temperature warning screen is displayed. If Apple Watch can't regulate its internal temperature, it goes into Power Reserve or a deep sleep mode until it cools. Move Apple Watch to a cooler location out of direct sunlight and wait a few minutes before trying to use Apple Watch again.

Magnets Keep key cards and credit cards away from Apple Watch, the bands, the Apple Watch Magnetic Charging Cable, and the Apple Watch Magnetic Charging Case.

23. THANK YOU FOR READING !

Thank You so much for reading this book. If this title gave you a ton of value, It would be amazing for you to leave a REVIEW !

THANK YOU FOR DOWNLOADING! IF YOU WOULD LIKE TO BECOME APART OF OUR READER COMMUNITY AND RECEIVE UPDATES ON UPCOMING TITLES PLEASE EMAIL PARAMOUNTPUBLISHINGCO@GMAIL.COM